# THE WAR BETWEEN THE WHIRLIGIGS AND THE TANKS

© Toni Lynn Chinoy, 1999

THE WAR BETWEEN THE WHIRLIGIGS
AND THE TANKS

COPYRIGHT © Toni Lynn Chinoy

This book may not be reproduced or distributed, in whole or in part, in print or by any other means without the written permission of the author. You can contact Toni Lynn Chinoy at toni@harlanevans.com.

ISBN 1-929910-00-2

CATAPULT PRESS, INC
P.O. BOX 32113
HILLSBORO, VA 20134-1613
(540) 668-7158

And so the Angel said to the Whirligig, "I don't understand. Why are you so angry with the Tanks? We sent them to protect you while you taught the world about magic."

## ACKNOWLEDGMENTS

I would like to express my appreciation to those who helped do the finishing work on this project. First my thanks to my husband, Marc, for modeling the Tank at its finest . Thanks go to Nancy Porter for being the editor in chief on this book, and to Jamie Kalvestran for, once again, creating the art to reflect my vision. Thank you to David Hopkins for his photography work for the back cover.

## TABLE OF CONTENTS

| | |
|---|---|
| CHAPTER I | WHAT'S A TANK? |
| CHAPTER II | WHAT'S A WHIRLIGIG? |
| CHAPTER III | WHAT'S THE PROBLEM? |
| CHAPTER IV | HOW DID THE FIGHTING START? |
| CHAPTER V | SYMPTOMS? |
| CHAPTER VI | WHY BOTHER? |
| CHAPTER VII | WHAT TO DO? |
| CHAPTER VIII | HARMONY AT LAST! |

## FOREWORD

Whirligigs and Tanks are phenomena of our social structure. They represent two extremes of our personality types and they reflect much of the discord occurring at a micro and a macro level. Whenever I speak of these two personality types to groups of people, the eyeballs roll in recognition and people pass meaningful looks to each other. It seems most of us have experienced the difficulties of the relationship between Whirligigs and Tanks.

It may seem an oversimplification to talk about many of the ills of our society in terms of these two styles, but think of this text symbolically rather than literally. Think of it as simply a lens for looking at relationships from a slightly different, perhaps helpful, perspective.

You will probably identify elements of both Whirligig and Tank personalities in your own actions. At times you will become a Whirligig or a Tank depending on the circumstance. You will, however, fall most frequently to one side of the scale or the other and should have very little problem naming yourself as a Whirligig or a Tank.

It won't matter if you aren't sure. When you are being a Tank, you will have issues with the Whirligigs around you and when you are being a Whirligig, you will have issues with the Tanks.

The purpose of this brief text is to create understanding about the two very different approaches to life, to identify ways to apply that understanding to personal situations, and then to extrapolate the concept to the larger understandings that affect our ability to resolve conflict on an ever widening circle. As you read this text, perhaps you will decide whether you are a Whirligig or a Tank, determine which of your relationship problems are because of the difference between the two perspectives on life, and try to determine better ways to live and work together in harmony.

# CHAPTER 1

## WHAT'S A TANK?

### (from the Tank's point of view)

"The world is difficult. I know this to be true. I must work hard and be disciplined if I am to have what I want. I'm very clear about what I want. I want to establish the kind of life that protects me from the vagaries and deceits of others. I will build security for my future and the future of those I care about, and I will plan it carefully.

"I do not like to fail. I know that without planning and forethought, failure is a real possibility, and I have no intention of allowing that to happen.

"I'm very deliberate. I do not do things lightly and I am very responsible. I do not believe in walking away when things do not work. I'm not afraid of hard work, and I have incredible staying power.

"Whirligigs think I'm stubborn and rigid. They do not understand that only through my hard work and dedication do they have the things they want. It is me who does the heavy lifting and carries the weight of the world on my shoulders. I am Atlas.

"I don't really believe in Magic. I'd like to, but let's be practical. If I wait for Magic to bring order into my life, I will be disappointed and still have to do the work. I've learned to never set myself up to be disappointed. That is a fool's game. And I am not a fool.

"Mankind is not very evolved. I'd like to believe life could be better and people could live in peace, but I know better. The nature of man is such that someone will always try to control everyone else, and it would be crazy not to try to protect yourself from that. I've long since stopped being hurt every time someone does something destructive or hurtful. I've learned to expect it.

"I'm not a crusader. I don't need to fix the world. I need to prepare for deceit and greed and protect myself and my loved ones against it.

"Because I'm prepared, it is rare that someone takes advantage of me. I always think through the possibilities, and I form all my relationships carefully. I prepare to protect myself from all contingencies.

"I am not naive. I am very loyal, but when someone takes advantage of me, it is as though they have declared war. At war, I know how to protect myself. I fight to destroy the other side because I know that they fight to destroy me. I will often know when they are preparing to go to war, and I will make a preemptive strike so that I am not destroyed.

"I'm not sure there is a heaven. If there were, how could life be so messed up? I trust in nothing I cannot see. I must live with 'what is' and 'what is' is very dangerous.

"It is difficult to wound me. Only those who become very close have that power and I choose them very carefully. I am quite capable of shutting down my emotions when I need to.

"I do not understand why Whirligigs find me so annoying. They say that I am an obstacle to progress. The only reason things get done around here is because of me. Progress is made from planning and following through. I am very good at progress. I am after all, a Tank."

# CHAPTER II

## WHAT'S A WHIRLIGIG?

(From the Whirligig's point of view)

"There's magic around here, I know it. All I have to do is think about what I want and it happens. I don't like to plan or struggle or think about all the potential consequences if I fail. I know I will succeed.

"Life is supposed to be effortless and if something is too much work, then I'm not supposed to be doing it. If I try something and it becomes too complicated or takes too much work, then I know that I'm supposed to move on to the next plan.

"Money is easy I never worry about being without. I create it when I know that I really need it and when I'm without, I assume I'm supposed to learn something. I'm not very good at saving because I know I will have what I need when I need it.

"Tanks think I'm a dreamer and that I'm impractical. They are sure that if they do not intervene I will implode. They are mystified when I am successful, because surely I know nothing about life.

"The angels whisper in my ear constantly, directing my energy, showing me what I must do. When I cannot hear them, it is because the Tanks are making too much noise. Tanks want to clip my wings because they are afraid I will somehow take them down with me when I fall.

"I know what it is like to reach too high, too soon. I have fallen many times. I will fall again. But the angels talk to me and I know that the fall is designed to show me what I missed.

"Each fall brings me closer to Perfection and if I try something and fall again, I will develop a rationale for what I was supposed to learn and then I will try again. I will listen better to the angels next time.

"Others sometimes try to take advantage of me. They think I don't know. They believe that Whirligigs are somehow so disconnected that they are oblivious to the plots of selfish, greedy people.

"Not so! I know when I am betrayed. I feel it instinctively. I am wounded, but I know that the betrayal is part of a plan. If I am wounded too much, I just fly away, leaving others to be confused behind me. 'How irresponsible,' they think. I seem very unpredictable, after all.

"But really, I'm not. Not for anyone willing to know the Whirligig. I stay until the pain is too great and then I leave. That is my story. I stay until the pain is too great and then I leave. If you want to understand a Whirligig, understand what gives me pain. And then, only then, will you be able to predict when I will leave.

"So what gives a Whirligig pain? Whirligigs love to grow. They thrive among others who love to grow. Whirligigs know that if you are going to grow, you have to fall sometimes. That's how it works. The fall teaches you. Pain for a Whirligig comes when the people we are closest to refuse to grow. Whirligigs hang on like ticks until the other person refuses to grow. Then we move on.

"I can hear my angels. Others are attracted to me because they sense that I can hear my angels. They want to hear the angels too. What others often do not understand is that you must be prepared to fall if you want to hear your angels. It is a little like those outward bound or wilderness exercises where you learn to trust by falling backwards into the group's arms. Unless you fall, you will never really know if you can trust. You have to fall to know that your angels will always catch you. At the end of the fall, you find what you were meant to know to begin with; that we are meant to trust and that trusting the voices in your head is the path to heaven.

"Many who come close to me because they suspect I can hear the angels are afraid that, if they are too close, they will fall with me. They don't believe anyone will catch them and that is so very scary. And yet they want to believe.

"They come close and then they become afraid. They try to stop me, but, if they succeed, they will ruin my ability to hear my angels and what they are attracted to will be lost. They want to hear their angels, but they are not willing to take the fall as a part of the listening.

They are afraid of the fall.

"Angels tell you it is appropriate to have high ideals. I have very high ideals. I believe the world is supposed to be heaven after all. People are meant to fall in love, stay in love and treat each other as gods and goddesses. People should honor each other and respect each others' talents, especially if they are different than their own. How very impractical I am!

"I'm confused by violence. It makes no sense to me. The act of deliberately hurting another is painful to watch. I can't imagine it. I defend myself, but I attack no one first. I am surprised when others attack me. I never expect it, even though it seems to happen to me frequently.

"We were never meant to be at war, or to be hungry, or to do violence to each other with our words and with our actions. I hurt deeply when I see the damage that is done, but I don't know how to stop it. I will try.

"I'm wounded when others do not understand who I am, when they think that I'm dangerous or impractical or perhaps even stupid. They treat me as though I do not understand life or the world or reality as they define it. They do not understand that I bring a gift and that I'm so very willing to share it freely with anyone who wants it. I am after all, a Whirligig."

# CHAPTER III

## WHAT'S THE PROBLEM?

The problems are infinite. There is a communication void between these two personality types that causes much of the stress we have in our working environments and in our marriages, and that stress ultimately has a significant impact on the world-at-large.

When a Tank and a Whirligig talk to each other, they often completely misunderstand the intentions and motives of the other. They are looking at the world from fundamentally different perspectives. Those perspectives, and the lack of appreciation for the differences found in those perspectives, causes much of the difficulty.

Below is what symbolically might be viewed as a typical conversation between a Whirligig and a Tank. You may recognize many of the issues as they unfold between these two.

# THE DIALOGUE

Whirligig: "I decided I don't like my profession any longer. I think I'll switch."

Tank: "What do you mean? Switch to what? When? How?"

Whirligig: "Oh, I don't know. I think I might like to do something different. I think I would really like to start a manufacturing company."

Tank: "What are you talking about? What's the product? What will it cost? Start a manufacturing company? That's so vague. You must be specific!"

Whirligig: "I'd like to own my own company. I want it to create a product that I can sell. I'll figure it out."

Tank: "Whirligig, do you have any idea what it takes to start something like that? Even if you did know what your product was, do you understand the years of planning and training it would take and the networks you would have to build? You would need financing and location and what makes you think the bankers and suppliers and everyone would take you seriously?"

Whirligig : "Well, I don't know all that, but I know that if I decide to do this, I'll just keep my mind open and the product will come to me. I'll figure the rest out as I need to."

Tank: "You've clearly got a screw loose. What about your career? What about all the training you have that doesn't have anything to do with building a company? Are you just going to give that up? How will you get the new training? How will you support yourself?"

Whirligig: "Who cares? I'm ready to do it now. I'll figure it out as I go. A person can do anything he or she sets his or her mind to. Besides, what good did all that training do our current leaders? Maybe a little less training and a little more understanding of how the world really works would have helped them. In terms of all my training so far, if I'm not happy why would I stay with it? That makes no sense at all."

Tank: "Look, if you insist on doing this, let me help you. I'll help you develop a plan. It might take a year or two, but it will be worth it, I promise. You won't make a fool of yourself when you get there and you won't go broke trying."

Whirligig : "Oh, no you don't. I know you. If I do it your way, we'll plan ad-nauseam and I'll never get there. The whole world will be different by the time I get ready to do anything and the plan will be useless. Everything takes so long with you."

Tank: "Well at least I don't make infinite mistakes and use up all my credibility trying to accomplish something that never had a prayer from the beginning. Remember that multi-level marketing firm you joined five years ago? You wasted all that time, not to mention the money you spent on the shelves of product you still own."

Whirligig: " I forgot about that. I guess I was

meant to own my own business all along. I must go back and examine everything I learned from that time. How lucky I am to have that experience now that I'm *really* ready to own my own company."

Tank: "Well what if you do figure out a product and get something started and it fails? And this time you really do it all the way? What if you go bankrupt? A lot of new businesses do, you know. Then what happens to you? Another dead end. Another wasted year or years. You can't keep doing this."

Whirligig: "How can you think that way? I wouldn't be at a dead end. I would have a new idea by then from all the things I was working on. I would have learned a lot more by doing it than I would have by spending my time planning it, and I would be so much smarter because I would already know what all the obstacles are. You would still be guessing and building contingencies for what might never happen. And besides, I would already know that it wasn't going to work and I wouldn't have spent two years building a plan. Seems to me I end up in the same place, but richer for the experience."

Tank: "It is beyond me how you survive."

Whirligig: "I know it is! It is beyond me how you ever get anything done."

✳ ✳ ✳ ✳ ✳

It should be obvious from the above conversation that the Whirligigs and the Tanks do things differently. They have very different views of the world and how to be successful. In certain circumstances, these differences can create a very positive complimentary relationship. Unfortunately, this is rarely the case. Too often, communication breaks down, progress stops, and enormous energy is expended in anger.

Because Whirligigs and Tanks are so often thrown together, they must learn to understand each other or pay the consequences.

The stakes can be high. A marriage can be the battleground. Many careers are affected by the battle of these two perspectives. At times, international issues may evolve into a crisis as a result of misunderstandings between the two styles.

When the two personalities clash, the Whirligig can suffer the ultimate disaster; a situation where he or she can not live out his or her dreams and fantasies. The Tank closes in and confines the Whirligig. That way the Whirligig cannot do any damage to the Tank's more practical and safe existence. The Whirligig may then feel like a caged animal, restless and angry, lashing out at anyone or anything that comes too close. The Tank, out of self-preservation, learns to put down the Whirligig's ideas as frivolous and foolish.

On the other side, the Tank is made to feel slow and useless. The Whirligig will often insert an element of chaos just when the Tank feels progress is about to be made. The Tank balks, and his or her courage often becomes the question mark. The war is in full play now. Each puts the other down and they are caught in the swirling impasse that results.

In either case, loss of self-esteem becomes the consequence. The two individuals each make the other feel as though the other can do nothing right. The Tank is "too slow" and the Whirligig is "irresponsible".

It is probable you have participated in Tank/Whirligig battles. They often start when you have an idea and the other side finishes it off before you get it out of your mouth. The Tanks spend hours arguing with the Whirligigs about the practicality of an idea, and Whirligigs spend hours trying to get people to just do something... anything.

The real problem is the result: No progress, numerous bodies on the battlefield, and a world that operates with the forward momentum of the caterpillar, two steps forward, one step back.

# CHAPTER IV

## HOW DID THE FIGHTING START?

Whirligigs and Tanks are excellent at triggering each other's anger. The anger is generally related to a fear. If you want to understand Whirligigs and Tanks and the complicated relationships that evolve between the two personalities, you will want to understand what makes them afraid. If either a Whirligig or Tank becomes afraid, they react intensely and will often create a lot of damage before the dust settles.

A Whirligig has one fear. The biggest fear for the Whirligig is of being hemmed in or trapped. Whirligigs are often ahead of their time, and frequently have visions of themselves beyond their maturity level. A Whirligig does not believe in paying dues. If a Whirligig believes that he or she is ready for a specific assignment or task, he or she will see no point in allowing the grey hairs to form or the years to accumulate.

If a Tank wants to keep the Whirligig on track and happy, he or she is wise never to attempt to capture or control the Gig. The

Tank is also exhibiting intelligence by never suggesting that the Whirligig is incapable of accomplishing any "hair-brained" idea. Any indication on the Tank's part that the Whirligig does not know or understand the implications of a plan will lead to an "in your face" exhibition of how wrong the Tank is. Those exhibitions can be costly to both Tanks and Whirligigs.

    The Whirligig can and does respond to dares. Comparatively, he or she is a bit reactive to statements or behaviors that indicate skepticism of a Whirligig intention. Above all, the Whirligig wants to be taken seriously and is quite sensitive to slights. The Tank, on the other hand, will often go out of his or her way to insult the Gig's ideas as incomplete, impractical, or even stupid. Each of these responses will make the Whirligig feel as if the Tank is using useless, biased responses to keep the Gig from moving forward.

    The Tank's fear, on the other hand, is of being out of control. The free-fall that the Whirligig is so comfortable with and actually seeks, is the Tank's nightmare. The Tank genuinely wants to know that actions have been well thought through, and he or she takes pride in identifying the potential pitfalls in any plan. The

Tank will spot a poorly planned initiative long before the Whirligig is finished talking.

Whirligigs often brainstorm out loud. Unfortunately, if they are challenged by the more thoughtful Tank, the Whirligig will insist that the brain impulse of the moment is something they have been thinking about for a very long time.

As the Whirligig digs in and insists that the idea is awesome, the Tank becomes convinced that the Gig is determined to destroy everything the Tank has worked for. If the Whirligig is allowed to attempt the thoughtless plan, the Tank believes he or she will be completely ruined. The Tank's response is appropriate to the level of impending destruction the Tank is assuming will happen.

Interestingly, the Tank is quite comfortable when others challenge his or her ideas. In fact, the Tank welcomes the challenges. Tanks love to have someone point out what might have been missed in the planning process because the Tank's ultimate objective is success. The Tank demands that any potential pitfall in the planning process be ruthlessly exposed. It is within the hidden obstacles that the Tank's fear resides.

Tanks hate to be surprised! They spend enormous energy attempting to insure that they won't be taken unaware. Because they take such pride in their ability to identify things that will go wrong *before* they happen, Tanks are offended and wounded when they miss something. It is not uncommon for a Tank to be completely disgusted at the thought of having missed some important detail that will cause problems later on.

There is another dynamic affecting the quality of the relationship between a Whirligig and a Tank. It is a sense of honor or trust. First, if the Tank insults the Whirligig by attacking a Whirligig idea, and the Whirligig is driven to prove the Tank wrong, the Whirligig is very likely to thrust forward with a half-formed plan. Something will go wrong and it is very likely to be something predictable. The Tank now has more ammunition for why the Whirligig must be stopped. The next plan meets with immediate skepticism and the Gig is ultimately trapped in a situation that is impossible for his or her free-spirited nature.

The next step is War. The Whirligig attacks the Tank and the Tank's uncompromising nature. The Tank, depending on his or her own need to be appreciated and to have peace, may be coerced into trying the next plan. But when it goes wrong, as Whirligig plans often do, the Tank feels as though he or she is on a roller coaster that is running out of control. The Tank begins to drag his or her feet and ultimately may balk. The Whirligig feels betrayed, since the Tank had agreed to cooperate, and all trust breaks down.

Is the Tank wrong? Probably not. Is the outcome the best outcome? Undoubtably, no! Perhaps the Whirligig idea has enormous merit but has not been through the necessary scrutiny to increase the odds for its potential to be realized.

Remember, the Whirligig has no fear of failure. When the inevitable errors occur, the Gig is fully prepared to drop back, assess, and step into the next iteration of the plan. Because the Gig reacts quickly to faltering plans, he or she often catches things in time before too much damage has been done.

The Tank, on the other hand, is usually not inclined to live terribly long with uncomfortable situations. He or she will step in quickly, stop all progress, and insist either that the idea was bad or that nothing more should happen until everything is fixed, or both.

Many times the Whirligig needs time to work out the bugs in an idea, since it is unlikely that the Gig will have planned for all contingencies. Unfortunately, because the Tank abhors failure, false starts are very upsetting. At the first sign of a problem, the Tank may want to bail out. This again creates a sense of betrayal for the Whirligig, since the Gig knows that with a few adjustments, the idea will work.

So, what is the real issue between these two? Ultimately, it falls to two main themes. The first theme is Trust, which in turn, resides within the second theme, which is the most important pivotal determiner of the success of the relationships between Whirligigs and Tanks .....RESPECT.

The war between the Whirligigs and the Tanks will continue until the end of time unless these two learn how to respect and honor and integrate their efforts with the talents and skills of the other. This integration must occur, both at a personal and at a global level. The next chapter talks about why.

# CHAPTER V

## SYMPTOMS?

Once we examine the symptoms of these Whirligig/Tank relationships gone bad, the need to change, and sometimes the way to change, becomes apparent.

### Tanks and Whirligigs in Love

At the most personal of levels, Whirligigs and Tanks are often attracted to each other. The Whirligig might meet and form relationships with other Whirligigs, but often those relationships are just too volatile for the vulnerable Whirligig. With both heads in the clouds, the actual work of solidifying the relationship might never be accomplished.

The Whirligig longs for someone who knows what he or she wants and knows how to get it. Where is that someone who follows through on commitments and finishes what gets started? Enough of these dreamers who are off chasing the next dream as soon as the first one has been articulated. Two Whirligigs can be very romantic together, but are often just a little too unstable to last.

What about the Tank? Tanks often find other Tanks quite comfortable to be with, but sometimes in a Tank/Tank relationship, one or both of the Tanks will still have his or her antennae up, looking for someone who can add a vitality often missing in a Tank/Tank relationship.

When the Tank and the Whirligig come together, it's Magic. The Tank loves the spontaneity of the Gig. Life and love goes from black and white to technicolor. The excitement of being with a Whirligig is energizing and somehow the most remote of the Tank's ambitions and dreams seems not just possible, but probable.

All of the Whirligig's prayers seem answered. The Tank clearly means what he or she says. Here is a person who appreciates the magic of the Whirligig. The Tank wants to listen to the Whirligig's dreams.

The two decide they are incredible

complements to each other: the doer and the dreamer. They forge a bond and formalize the relationship. And then the trouble begins.

The Whirligig continues to chase the dreams and the Tank is completely destabilized. "Well, yes, I wanted to create Nirvana in our back yard, but I thought that was years down the road. First we have to level the ground, and fertilize, and prepare....".

"But I thought you meant now. I'm ready now. I can't wait five years."

Issue after issue surfaces. Soon the Whirligig feels trapped and wishes for the solitary life where there was no one to interfere. Freedom seems so appealing. The prior life, with all of the loneliness and the despair of the failed relationships, is forgotten. Freedom becomes the big fantasy.

The Whirligig has made a promise to the Tank. If the Whirligig has honor, he or she feels even more despair and more hopelessness than before when the Whirligig was just lonely. There is no way out. The promise must be kept, but life feels empty and meaningless.

When the Whirligig attempts to adapt to

the new situation, it is like a wild bird adapting to a cage. Occasionally the old spirit resurfaces and a new idea will form and is articulated, but it is not long before the Tank feels out of control and will step in to stop the momentum. Any reprieve for the Whirligig from the intense emotional despondency is brief.

Soon, sadness becomes a part of the Whirligig's expression whenever the Gig is with his or her Tank. Trust for the Tank becomes history. After all, the Tank broke the biggest promise of all, the promise to nurture the Whirligig's spirit.

At times the Tank is surprised to see the joyful expression of the Gig's animated face as he or she converses with other Gigs who understand. The Tank feels a tug but does not know how to respond. It makes the Tank happy to see the old expression back on the face of the beloved, but what to do about it?

The Tank ignores the feelings struggling inside, because to delve into them means to open a Pandora's box which is certain to threaten the safety of the Tank's carefully constructed world.

And what does the Tank feel? He or she also feels betrayed. After all, the Tank has done nothing wrong. He or she has, at all times, acted with integrity. The Tank is only trying to protect the two of them. Why is that so unappreciated?

It seems that the Tank is not allowed to say "no" to the Whirligig without a scene. There are many potential conversations that never happen that could create more understanding between the two. The Tank is reluctant to start the conversation because he or she might incur the wrath of the Gig. The Tank hesitates, and the Whirligig will always sense the Tank's unspoken hesitation. The Gig will force a conversation about the Tank's reluctance, and then the predictable scene occurs.

Sometimes the Whirligig will simply not ask the Tank. After all, if the Tank has chosen not to make an issue of whatever is now on the table, the Tank must have no preferences. The Gig assumes cooperation and launches into projects affecting both of them without ever checking with the Tank.

The Tank can't seem to win. The Gig

thinks the Tank is a slug with no imagination. At times, the Whirligig becomes a spoiled child who insists on having his or her way. The more trapped the Whirligig becomes, the more childlike and immature are his or her responses. The Tank, a perfectly rational human, feels cornered into living an unpredictable, chaotic life that has no elegance. Over time, the Tank becomes angry and short-tempered. Combined with the Whirligig's sadness, this picture becomes quite bleak.

At first, they handle the dilemma with humor. They may joke about the incidents. Over time the humor takes on an edge and the Tank begins to make disparaging comments about the Whirligig's various adventures, while the Whirligig makes fun of the Tank's lack of flair. The Tank stops supporting the Gig and then waits for the adventures to turn into failures. When they do, the Tank loves to tell the stories, again and again. Unfortunately, the Tank rarely notes when the Whirligig approach has uncanny timing and, occasionally, brilliant success. The Tank only counts the failures, since that is the Tank's biggest concern.

Successes are often just "good luck", nothing more.

And so the Tank points out the flaws in the Gig's approach. The Gig becomes offended. He or she reacts by defending the actions taken and the rationale for why that path was the only choice. Whirligigs often find themselves talking about the circumstances that caused the breakdown of the plan as if they were all out of the Gig's control.

Left to his or her own devices, the Whirligig would be philosophical about the failure. It is the natural way of the Whirligig to simply examine the problem and determine the next steps. However, when faced with the Tank's criticism, the Gig becomes defensive and takes the tone of a victim.

The Tank becomes more derisive. It soon becomes uncomfortable to spend time with the two of them because the conversation becomes disrespectful. Friends see the value of both their friends' approaches, yet they have no idea how to help these two begin to appreciate each other again.

# Tanks and Whirligigs at Work

Even if you were not fortunate enough to have chosen your opposite personality style for your primary relationship, it is possible, in fact, even probable, that you have run into the obstacles created by these two perspectives in your professional life.

In the workplace, Tanks and Whirligigs are the cause of frequent stand-offs around initiatives. What are some of the symptoms of a Whirligig/Tank problem at the office?

Surprisingly, the first symptom of a Whirligig/Tank battle is about process. The issue is about how the two conduct themselves. The Tank will often complain of wasted time in meetings. He or she will usually be the one who insists that an agenda be created and then managed in order to make meetings more productive.

Tanks want to know what will be discussed for two basic reasons. Remember, Tanks don't like to be surprised. They never want to look foolish. The Tank wants to be prepared. The Tank is the one who will actually do his or her homework before the meeting.

The second reason the Tank wants an agenda is because he or she does not want the Whirligig to take the meeting off on some wild tangent that serves no useful purpose. The Tank assumes that an agenda will control a Whirligig.

In an organization where meetings run like clockwork, the Whirligigs will often wistfully comment that they wish they could have meetings from time to time where people just explored new ideas. The very thought of such a meeting might make the Tank hyperventilate.

It is important to differentiate between having meetings that run like clockwork and having a successful organization. Tanks often live with the myth that if everything is in order and runs with precision, the organization will be successful. The truth is that the Tanks in such an organization may be more comfortable, but it does not mean that profitability automatically follows.

And so, process, as an issue between Whirligigs and Tanks, is important. Tanks especially need predictability in processes around professional issues. Whirligigs need variety and freedom of expression.

After process, the next issue of diversity between the two styles is a fundamental difference in terms of how they think the world, and therefore business, works.

The Whirligig feels his or her way through the professional world. Intuition is a major force in determining the Whirligig's next steps. The Whirligig will often have flashes of insight and will base huge initiatives on a momentary vision. The Whirligig is often sketchy about explaining why he or she absolutely knows that he or she is heading in the right direction.

The Tank does not like to base anything on what might be called a whim. It makes Tanks very uncomfortable to think that critical resources are being allocated based on a flash of inspired thinking.

You've been in the meeting when this happens. The Whirligig has just stated with absolute certainty that he or she knows exactly what should happen next. Unfortunately, the Tank can't make the intuitive leap with the Gig. Instead of trying, the Tank often likes to point out all the reasons the Gig plan will never work.

At this point, because the Tank has not had the time to properly examine the Gig's idea, he or she will focus on fear-based obstacles to the Gig's ideas. This tendency reaffirms the Gig's impression that the Tank is a fearful creature looking for bogeymen.

### A. *Whirligig in Charge*

Rank creates some interesting dynamics for Whirligigs and Tanks at work. If the Whirligig happens to hold the higher position, the subordinates will often fall into two camps. The first camp loves working with the Whirligig. Life is exciting, change is constant and the new directions are ones that differentiate the Gig's organization as one of leadership. If the Gig is respectful of the Tank's ability to identify potential pitfalls, the Tank is grateful to be on the cutting edge of his or her profession.

The second camp is, unfortunately, the one that occurs more often. In this scenario, the Tank is unhappy because the change comes too fast. He or she can never feel prepared and life feels out of control. Often the Tank becomes subversive. The Tank may start by openly opposing his or her boss. The Whirligig's ego is not cut out for open criticism. If the Tank is too aggressive, the Gig is quite capable of embarrassing the Tank publically. Soon the Tank operates more subtly, but the intention is to stop the Gig before the Gig gets everyone in trouble.

A CEO of a small company was a Whirligig. He was hired to turn around a troubled business. He immediately saw that the organization was doing many things very well but that the nature of the industry itself had changed dramatically since the employees had learned their skills. While they were doing what they had learned to do exceptionally well, the business was steadily losing money and market share.

The Gig was quick to identify where the business needed to be and to begin creating new product. He also improved the cost structure on the fundamental business that had been the foundation for the company's success in the past. He found that people had stopped thinking about what they were doing, and instead were doing things based on procedures. The customers felt like numbers and were going elsewhere with their business.

Unexpectedly for the Tanks, initial results

were staggering. The organization went quickly to a profitable and eventually highly successful example of what could be done in a changing industry.

The employees, Tanks and Gigs alike, loved being a part of the experience. Who doesn't like winning after a long losing streak? And then the trouble began.

After several consistent years of exceptional growth and performance, the Gig continued doing what he had done from the beginning. He continued to throw one idea after another over the wall. After several years of extraordinary performance, the Tanks who worked for him had had enough. They were no longer afraid and they were no longer hungry. They were tired of being stretched to the limits of their comfort zone. They wanted to stabilize.

They were worried. They could no longer support putting new ideas into play. They wanted to build systems to support all of the new ideas they were working with already.

They tried to tell the Whirligig that they had reached their capacity for change. The Gig didn't hear them. They tried criticizing the ideas. The Gig got annoyed. They tried dragging their feet and talking to each other at the water cooler about how unhappy they were. The Gig became impatient. Where were all the soldiers he had come to count on during the war?

And that's the problem. Whether looking at the specific history mentioned above, or at any situation where the Whirligig is in charge, Whirligigs can be incredibly visionary. They often know just what to do when everyone else is vacillating. They are enthusiastic and good at leading a charge. They can be great leaders, particularly in difficult times. They are, after all, fearless and decisive when things are in crisis. They are refreshing.

Unfortunately, they don't always wear well over time. Whirligigs are the same whether at war or at peace. When the danger is past, their enthusiasm can be draining . The Gig continues to seek and embrace change. When others are ready to rest, the Gig charges on.

After a time, people realize that some of the Gig's ideas just don't work. They are great in theory but perhaps they miss some critical element. The Tanks are judgmental about the failures. They soon forget that they may have been failing before the Gig arrived. It isn't always just a failed idea; it is sometimes a failing business. They soon forget about the successful ideas the Gig has implemented, as they clean up the ideas that don't succeed.

Whirligigs in charge are often sprinters. They sprint for the line and then they must step back and rest. In the meantime, the Tanks, who have much greater stamina, are left doing the heavy lifting. They resent the Gig's frequent rest periods. Soon, there is little appreciation left for the Gig's brilliance. All the Tanks can see is that the Gig is acting like spoiled royalty. The ship begins to resemble the Bounty and the crew prepares to mutiny.

B. *The Tank Has the Rank*

If the Tank holds the higher position, the dynamics are slightly different but equally destructive.

The Tank will be very linear in his or her expectations, and the Whirligig is not a linear person. The Tank still does not like surprises and because Whirligigs are such spontaneous personalities, they will often take the Tank unawares.

The Tank's response is often to impose procedures and controls on the Gig. The Gig will feel trapped, angry, and frustrated. Gigs work best and most effectively with a lot of freedom. They will often create results far beyond the expectations of the Tank if allowed to have their head. Their methods will often be disorganized and lack logical progression, but this does not mean they are ineffective.

Take for example, the Whirligig who became, for the first time in her life, a computer hardware sales person. She went through the very sophisticated sales training, and then went out and started knocking on the doors of small businesses, which was her territory. Within a very short period of time, she had over a half a million dollars worth of prospects seriously interested in her product. She began spending time in the office, talking with these prospects on the phone and networking within the organizations she had penetrated.

The senior sales manager was a Tank. He saw the amount of time the Gig was spending in the office and became concerned. The Tank believed strongly, from his experience, that new sales reps need a lot of discipline. They will *only* be successful if they follow a certain pattern. The pattern consists of a specific number of cold calls by phone, a specific number of attempts to knock on doors, etc....

He called the Gig into his office and proceeded to scold her for being in the office too much. When she started to explain what was happening with her business, he interrupted and handed her a form for cold calls. On the form she was to list each phone call, the time of day, the contact, and their response to her call. There was also a segment for listing businesses that she called on personally for the first time. Without listening to her attempts to inform him of what was happening with her territory, the manager told her that she was to completely fill out the list each week and would be measured against how complete her lists were.

The Gig was completely disgusted. First, the rigid format was not something she could follow without becoming completely drained of energy. Secondly, the process made such poor business sense to her because it defeated the purpose of what she thought she was supposed to do and be. She lost respect for the Tank.

The Gig will often have insights beyond the step by step sequence the Tank likes to follow and, as a result, will become impatient with following the Tank. Why follow a path the Gig deems to be worthless?

In this situation, the Whirligig was approached by a head-hunter about another sales job. She took it.

She tried to do the 'right' thing. She gave her old company several weeks of her time to teach the sales manager about what she had been working on. When the sales manager realized how much potential business she had generated in a short time, he was amazed. He could not believe that she had been able to do so much, and that he was losing her.

"Why didn't you tell me you had all this business in the pipeline?" he asked incredulously. "How in the world did you generate this so quickly?"

"I tried to tell you when you insisted I fill out these stupid cold call sheets," she said. "I was so afraid I would lose contact with these people who were really interested while I was calling on companies that had not expressed any interest. I hope you don't lose this business because I haven't had much time to follow up on it."

She was able to help him close a good deal of the business and they both learned something. The manager learned that he needed to become less rigid, and the Whirligig learned that she really needed to think about working for herself.

The relationship described above is not unusual for a working relationship in which a Tank is in charge of a Whirligig. The Tank will often attempt to create discipline in the Whirligig, a somewhat awesome task. The Whirligig will often chafe under the control of the Tank. Eventually, the communications fall apart. The costs are considerable.

## *Whirligigs and Tanks on Global Issues*

The dynamics are the same whenever you have Whirligigs and Tanks working or playing together. Whether these personalities are running a multibillion dollar corporation, an ice cream shop, or are world leaders making decisions for our future, the personality differences exist and affect the relationships.

If you remember that we all have elements of both types within our personalities, it is easier to understand why we always have Gigs and Tanks working together on important issues. Different circumstances will bring out the Gig in one and the Tank in another. Often an extreme Tank will bring out the Whirligig in a Tank-like personality. Or the opposite may be true. An extreme Whirligig may cause the most free-spirited person to become Tank-like.

Perhaps it is destiny that determines who plays in the positions of power at any given moment. There is no rule that the highest leadership positions will be either Whirligig or Tank. He or she can and will be either.

For example, George Bush would probably fall on the side of a Tank. Bill Clinton is definitely a Whirligig. Margaret Thatcher might be a Tank. They all have very different styles of responding to crisis.

Bill Clinton can change on a dime and reinvent his approach moment to moment. As a Whirligig, he would not think that this style was the least bit illogical. It only makes sense to be prepared to change direction if the current plan is not working (assuming there is a plan). This is not necessarily bad. It would mean that President Clinton would be much more in touch with and adaptable to the public opinion than would a Tank. For the Tanks of the world, however, he would seem erratic and frightening. Whirligigs might find his approach refreshing.

A Tank in a position of extreme power, on the other hand, would be much more likely to be oblivious to the reactions of others to his or her actions. The Tank will often justify his or her lack of results by falling back on the Plan. The Plan rules. Woe unto he or she who attempts to change the direction established by the Tank in the middle of executing his or her Plan.

Examine the last two major conflicts in which the U.S. has engaged from the perspective of analyzing the difference of approach between a Whirligig and a Tank. Do you see a difference?

Is the approach of George Bush methodically enlisting the alliance of world leaders for the Gulf War not different than the approach of the Clinton administration to the war in Kosovo? The one was a very analytical, aggressive response to an invasion of Kuwait from Iraq. On the other hand, the war the U.S. waged against the Serbian Army was clearly an emotional and moral response to human rights issues. The administration was criticized for having no plan and for being in a strictly reactionary mode.

Whether these are accurate assessments is not the point. The point is that the Whirligigs of the world were saying, "Right on!" to Madeline Albright's concerned, humanistic response to the situation. The Tanks were horrified and wanted to know, "What's the plan? What's the exit strategy?"

During the Gulf War, it was the Whirligigs who were horrified. "Why are we doing this? How can we justify killing all these people?" The Tanks applauded the war as a demonstration of the advantages of fighting a technological war. Whirligigs were very unconcerned about the advantages of technology. That's a Tank thing.

By understanding the differences in the styles of our world leaders, could we begin to anticipate some of the kinds of responses they might have during a crisis? Perhaps we could even begin to diminish the number of crises if we understood the things that would trigger a fear-based response in a leader.

Why? What does fear have to do with world issues? Remember that the Whirligigs and Tanks each have specific things that cause fear reactions. A Whirligig is afraid of being controlled or a loss of freedom. Whirligigs also hate to be discounted in any way. If the Whirligig is caused to fear for his or her freedom, or to fear that he or she is not being taken seriously, the response is likely to be dramatic. How often have we initiated serious world dramas because a Whirligig was discounted as irrelevant or erratic? Who knows? Perhaps we should start paying attention.

Or the Tank. Have we inadvertently caused the Tank to stop forward momentum because we were neglectful of keeping him or her informed on what might be deemed 'minor detail' by a Whirligig? Could we have some Tanks in our Congress who resent having initiatives started without having been consulted?

Which style is better? Would you rather have a Whirligig in charge or a Tank? The

Tanks reading this book, at this point, are very likely saying, "Why, it is obvious that the Tank's way of being is much more effective."

The Whirligig, who is often more prone to self-doubt than the Tank, might be thinking, "I know a Whirligig would be better. They're so much more attuned to human suffering than Tanks. I know I'm right, but what if I'm wrong?"

The real answer is that neither would necessarily be better or worse. One style will create a surrounding group of the opposite style. If the two groups, Whirligigs and Tanks, could learn to respect and utilize each other fully, we would always get the optimum result. The challenge is to understand that we have much to offer each other and to work with the potential of the situations created by Whirligigs and Tanks together.

## CHAPTER VI

## WHY BOTHER?

We should do the work of healing these relationships because we need each other. The Whirligigs need the Tanks and the Tanks need the Whirligigs. We need the Whirligigs to create magical visions of what the future can be and we need the Tanks to implement the visions. We need the Gigs to teach us about the world they live in, a world with no limits. We need the Tanks to ground us so that we can deal with reality, even as we create our magical future.

Without the Whirligig, the world loses vitality and purpose. Life becomes an endless process of 'getting by' and 'making do' with 'what is'. We need the Gig to stretch us and make us reach for what seems impossible, for how else will we ever know what we are capable of being and doing?

The Tanks can teach us to conserve and to guard what is precious. The Tank will help us to understand the value of what we have built.

Without the Tank, the Gig is predisposed to throw away what has been established, good or bad. No matter what, the Gig must keep moving.

For the Gig, a world of Tanks is too stale and too boring to be imagined. For the Tank, a world of Whirligigs is too chaotic to be contemplated. A world of these two personalities side by side can be either a world filled with conflict or a world of vital, pulsing energy, growing always toward the greatest harmony and most peaceful integration with the Universe. Such a world represents, in fact, what is meant to be.

If the Tank and the Gig could learn to work and live together, no matter who is in charge, what would be different?

Imagine a marriage between a Gig and a Tank where the two worked in constant harmony and mutual respect. The Tank has overcome his or her fear of change. He or she has learned to trust the insights of the Whirligig and the Gig's ability to predict the future. The Tank asks, "What should we do with the unexpected money we got back from the taxes?" and the Gig says, "Let's build a swimming pool and put the rest in the stock market."

The Tank says, "I don't know. That seems a little risky to me."

So the Gig says, "Okay. I think the pool will act like an investment because it adds to the value of our property. So we'll let that be the high risk portion of the investment because you never know if the market will be up or down or if pools will be in or out when we get ready to sell. So then the rest we should put in something more secure, like bonds or something. That way, we get to enjoy the money by enjoying the pool, we get to invest it in our asset of our house, and we are putting something away for the future that is not in a risky investment."

The Tank agrees and the two move forward with their plans. The Tank carefully lays out a plan for the swimming pool and shops for the appropriate contractor. The Tank does the research and chooses the appropriate bonds. The Gig makes the decisions that need to be made regarding materials for the pool and makes the final intuitive choice between the two bonds the Tank is recommending.

The two blend their skills and trust each other with the parts of the decisions that reflect their strengths. The Whirligig makes the intuitive decisions. The Gig trusts that the research must be done, but the Tank trusts the Gig's insight during the decision-making process. If the Gig comes with a new idea indicating a change for the two of them, the Tank trusts enough to do the research to validate the idea.

When they go to sell the house, swimming pools are "In". That's how it works with Gigs. Their swimming pool has been extremely well planned and laid out. That's how it is with Tanks.

The Gig acts as a trusted advisor to the Tank. The Tank can't see the future as well as the Gig and he or she knows it. So when the Tank is trying to decide on whether or not to change jobs, he asks the Gig for advice. The Gig gives the Tank a wide range of options and the Tank considers each of the options.

This potential would be no different in the world of work. If the Tank and the Whirligig could learn to enhance each other's strengths and to offset each other's weaknesses, we would see vital, thriving organizations rather than organizations mired in discussion and impasse.

Globally, we could also create change for the positive, if only the Whirligig and the Tank could learn to communicate and strategize together. The Gigs could create positive visions of what life on this planet could and should be like, and the Tanks could develop the systems and structures to support the change.

Within our current levels of misunderstanding, unfortunately, progress is impeded through wasted energy as the personalities fight each other.

The Tank, while more methodical and patient about achieving an end result, can often devote too much time and too much energy to a plan that will not work. Reluctant to shift gears in midstream, a Tank may become obstinate about something which could have a long term negative impact on an organization, or a family, or an entire ecosystem. The Whirligig, on the other hand, may have a brilliant idea but lack the ability to create and stick to a plan. Because the Whirligig can change directions so easily, because he or she is comfortable with the idea of a plan failing from time to time, and because the Gig is constantly creating new directions, the end result may be a constantly shifting target.

Businesses run by Tanks generally concentrate on building systems, maintaining customer bases, and generally improving the fundamentals of what exists. Businesses or organizations run by Whirligigs often concentrate on vision, reinventing, and creating change. There are times when the Tank's approach is not enough, and there are times when the Whirligig's style of creative chaos is inappropriate.

Neither circumstance is static. The answer that is right for one set of conditions will undoubtably change over time. A business which intensely needs revitalizing, a Whirligig speciality, will soon need the meticulous care and attention of the Tank to stabilize the innovations the Whirligig brings in. The Tank and the Gig need each other and need to admit it. We should all learn to know which circumstance calls for the Tank approach and which calls for the Whirligig's talents and then we must learn to support each other in those circumstances and move the ball back and forth as the situation continues to evolve.

# CHAPTER VII

## WHAT TO DO?

Start with an assumption that progress only occurs because of a blending of the diversity of these two styles. The Gig keeps things leaping forward and the Tank is bringing along the wealth and knowledge of the past. As in all aspects of nature, the Universe is set up perfectly. We must understand It's laws and then we will find the existence we were meant to enjoy .

So how do we begin working through the issues in order to learn to work together and take advantage of the wonderful potential?

### *Healing the Past*

The starting place is the past. We Tanks and we Whirligigs have a history together and much of it is not pleasant. There are wounds and battle scars that we can each trot out at any provocation. We love to revisit and retell the stories of all the ways we have been abused by the other side.

We must all recognize that we have caused these wounds and that we are not starting at ground zero. The Whirligigs have insulted the Tanks many times. The Whirligig's natural tendency to call the Tank names seems "all fair" during the fight, but the logical Tank, who would never use name-calling as a tactic, will remember forever the names the Gig has chosen.

The Tank, on the other hand, goes right for the throat. Rather than some inappropriate name describing a variety of ills, the Tank has probably pointed out on numerous occasions every one of the Gig's past failures. Never mind if the Tank has had similar failures. Those don't count.

The Tank may have used the Gig's failures as evidence of the Gig's incompetence. Because the Gig desires, above everything besides freedom, to be taken seriously, the Tank's use of Whirligig failures to indicate incompetence is unforgivable to the Gig.

Both sides have wounds they are still nursing, wounds that have led to a breakdown of trust between the two. The only way to move past the stalemate is for the Tank and the Whirligig to talk about their feelings.

The Tank has lost faith in the Gig's abilities because of a failure or a group of failures. The Gig must try to create for the Tank an understanding of the Gig perspective. The Gig must describe what the Gig was thinking while events were playing out. Often the Gig has a wonderful view of how the failure has repositioned the Gig in a very powerful and constructive way. The Tank benefits from hearing how the Gig looks at the world from the positive rather than the negative perspective of the failure.

The Tank must listen openly to understand why the failure does not mean that the Gig is incompetent. Instead the Tank should try to understand how the Gig views risk.

If the two are to heal the wounds they have inflicted on each other, the Tank is responsible for understanding that risk is often necessary for progress. The Gig may have taken a risk that is incomprehensible, but still admirable, from the point of view of a Tank.

If the Tank is capable of conceding an admirable trait in the Gig, the Gig must understand that the slow, methodical sequencing of steps necessary from the Tank's point of view does not make the Tank a "slug", a "jerk", an "idiot", or any other name the Gig may have chosen in a desperate attempt to break through the Tank's opinionated reserve.

The Gig must step back and find the traits to admire in the Tank. He or she must look for evidence of occasions when the Tank has been right, when methodical preparation, while consuming more time, has, in fact, saved the day.

The first step in resolving the issues is to heal the wounds, and the way to heal the wounds is for either side to contemplate the value of the other side's approach. First, one acknowledges the benefits to oneself. And then the acknowledging must be out loud. It is the only place to start.

## Rewriting the Expectations

The next step in re-framing the relationship of Tanks and Whirligigs is to examine where old wounds are creating expectations for current and future interactions.

We have all experienced the chaos caused by an out of control Whirligig, just as we have all experienced the sluggishness of the risk-averse planning processes of extreme Tankism. We begin to recognize and react to the symptoms. We have learned to have expectations, based on experience, that may or may not be accurate.

Our expectation triggers a behavioral reaction. The minute a Tank expresses reserve to a Whirligig, who has long suffered the delays of Tankdom, the Gig digs in, thinks of the names he or she would apply to the Tank, and prepares to go to war. The Gig misses on two counts. He or she could have over-reacted to a valid concern that may save a lot of re-work at some point in the future. Also, the Gig has just insured that the Tank will now do everything in his or her power to stop the process before it gets out of control.

Had the Gig waited, listened and then responded by asking the Tank to elaborate on the concern, two things would have happened.

The Tank would have developed less real resistance to the plan, and the Gig might have valuable information for moving forward.

In the moment when the Tank expressed concern, the Gig should have stopped and said internally, "Just because this Tank has a concern does not mean that everything will stop. That is something I may have experienced under other circumstances, but it does not have to happen this time. Instead, maybe I should expect that the Tank sees something I can't see from my position in the Universe and the Tank really just wants to help me."

In other words, the Gig becomes much more inclined to assume, "the Tank is my ally. He or she is my ground person, calling out the realities I cannot see from my position, just as I see things the Tank cannot see."

When the Whirligig operates from this perspective, the reactions are much more respectful of the Tank's issues. The Tank sees less to resist because the Tank does not feel as if he or she is being dragged headlong into a disaster. There is no longer a need for the Tank to dig in, and the dynamic of the interaction changes dramatically simply because the

Whirligig chooses to start with an expectation that the Tank was sent to protect the Gig.

The Tank also needs to reexamine expectations. Based on the past, he or she has come to expect that the Whirligig's plan of the moment has little likelihood of reaching completion and under worst circumstances may cause the Tank a mess to clean up. The Tank has become unable to respond to the merit of the idea itself, and instead reacts to past experiences. The Tank is not open and will immediately begin to throw out road blocks with very little reflection on whether the idea is positive or negative.

Suppose instead the Tank says quietly, "Whirligigs have been known to have extraordinary ability to find ponies where others see manure. It is possible that this new idea has the potential to change my world for the better. I'm going to look for the value that might be missed by others who are less open."

Coming from this perspective, the Tank is thoughtful when listening to the Gig and asks intelligent, provoking questions to better understand what the Gig really means. The Whirligig feels less need to defend the idea. He or she is naturally more open to the Tank's potential obstacles because they are delivered as things to think about rather than as reasons to toss the idea aside.

The following sections will offer specific do's and don't's for Gig/Tank interactions. You might want to memorize them, but if Tanks and Gigs work at changing expectations for their interactions, the behaviors will flow naturally. When they operate from a positive expectation, Gigs and Tanks will automatically create the harmony and the beauty of naturally complementary perspectives.

### Never say....to a Tank

If you want to increase your odds of positive and harmonious relationships between Tanks and Whirligigs, it is often wise to avoid certain types of interactions. The Tank and the Whirligig can be somewhat predictable in their responses to specific triggers. You might find it beneficial to memorize them.

The following are a few no-no's when dealing with a Tank:

- Never tell a Tank you were too busy to check your facts. In fact, never tell a Tank that you just have a "feeling" about important details. Offer instead to do the research and report back, or, better yet, figure out what research the Tank would do and do it before he or she asks.
- Never convey a sense of urgency based on fear to a Tank. It only creates the opposite reaction you are hoping for in the Tank. The Tank will slow down rather than speed up.
- Try to tone down your enthusiasm for a course of action. Enthusiasm automatically makes the Tank suspicious. He or she immediately assumes you are working from emotion rather than logic. Tanks have a huge mistrust of emotional decisions. Try instead to act as though you don't care either way, but that it (whatever it is that you are trying to sell) might be an interesting idea to pursue.
- When a Tank throws out an

obstacle, never 'shoot from the hip' with your response. It will only cost you credibility. Do not react, other than to say that you want to check into his or her concern and you will get back. Whirligigs who pretend the issue is irrelevant or attempt to persuade the Tank that it is unimportant, without doing the homework, sometimes lose huge battles they would otherwise win.

- Never ask a Tank for an immediate decision. They like to prepare their responses. When asked for an immediate decision, they will often automatically say no because it is safer to do so. Ask the Tank to think about the idea. The Tank will think about an idea if you give them time. What comes back may be unrecognizable, but you'll probably at least feel progress.

- Never assume that you are right. Assume you have the correct general direction, but that you need the Tank to help you see the pitfalls and alternatives you may have missed. Keep your attention on the essence of what you want to do, and use the Tank to help you find the most viable option to create that essence.

- In personal relationships, don't call the Tank names when you get upset as a way of getting the Tank's attention. The Tank will remember the name for the rest of your relationship. Be sure that you only say things that you would not be uncomfortable hearing repeated back to you for the next several years. The Tank responds much better to logic and facts.

- Never get hooked on one aspect of your plan. Go back to the essence of what you are trying to create. This is the hardest recommendation for Whirligigs to follow. You may be convinced that the way to save the company is for you to lobby the Congress to change the laws in your favor. You might be right. But the Tank knows what it takes to move a Congress and he or she will not bet their future on your fabulous persuasive talents. Instead, sneak your real idea in amidst a few practical, easily implemented ideas, and do not place an emphatic assertion out there that this is the idea that will save the company. You might say for example, "We could reassess our market, expand ourproduct line to meet the demands, and by the way, we might want to throw some resources into lobbying Congress to change that law, just in case."

- Don't attack a Tank's inability to follow you through the risk taking. They are not always saying that the idea is crazy. They are often simply telling you that they know that the idea would never work for *them.*

## Never say... to a Whirligig

The Whirligig also has a few triggers you might want to avoid. Unless you like experiencing the "wrath of the Gig", which is a little like experiencing a tornado, you might want to avoid the following potential weather builders:

- Never tell a Whirligig an idea is

a BAD IDEA. They hate that. For whatever reason, the Gig thinks you have insulted his or her intelligence. Instead, try finding the merit in the idea and suggesting a slightly different path which includes the essence of what the Gig has in mind. Another option is to attempt to discover, gently, what the Gig was hoping to accomplish with the idea. Your curiosity will enchant the Gig and they may actually say something that does get your respect.

- Never tell a Gig that an idea won't work without first telling the Gig what you liked about it. It is a sign of disrespect to do so.
- Never tell a Whirligig you have already tried something and it didn't work. The Gig will become convinced that there is a nuance to his or her idea that you are not considering and that it failed before because *you* were implementing it. To tell a Gig you already tried it and it failed simply convinces the Whirligig that you really never understood the idea in the first place and that's why it failed. Try

instead to indicate specific aspects of the idea that have failed and the need to find ways to work around those aspects and solve those problems before moving forward with a similar plan. The Gig would take that approach as a challenge and the Gig likes nothing more than to be considered as a resource for solving old problems that could not be solved previously. Besides, the Whirligig may just come up with a solution. If the idea was good enough to try before, perhaps it could be built on with the imagination and creativity of the Gig.

- Don't bring up past failures as a way of proving to the Whirligig that a new approach will fail. First the Gig does not regard the past mis-steps as failures. As far as the Gig is concerned, those are still plans in process. Also, it will make the Gig lose respect for you because it will seem like flak sent out to divert the Whirligig from his or her purpose. It is critical to understand that a Gig with a purpose is a force to be reckoned with.

- Do not attempt to make the Gig think you are a risk taker if you are not. Instead explain what your biggest fears are, and ask the Whirligig to identify solutions to your concerns. If you confess a fear to a Gig with a request for a potential solution, a Gig will respect you much more than if you pretend you have no fear but that the idea is faulty. You may find that the Whirligig's response actually helps you to see past a risk-averse position and to see the potential benefits from stepping into space.

## *Letting Go of Being Right*

This particular step applies to both Tanks and Whirligigs. It is about ego. Assume that no matter what side you are on, on any given issue, you might be wrong. Assume that you may be missing an important perspective that will help your personal situation enormously. Look at your life. Is it perfect? Have all of your decisions been flawless? Could you have used a balancing perspective?

Could you be more successful than you are now? If you are already as successful as you can ever imagine being, you probably should insist on having your way under all circumstances. But if there is any hesitation, any dream unfulfilled, assume the other side (Whirligig or Tank) just might have the answer to that unfulfilled dream. Take that other perspective and shake it like a tree until you think you have all the fruit off the branches, and then, shake it again.

Proving the Gig was wrong to pursue an idea is easier than proving that the Tank was wrong in avoiding it. You may never know how many opportunities you've missed, but you will always know when an idea fails. That is the magic and the curse of the relationship.

If the Whirligig and the Tank each let go of being right, the Gig can stop justifying failures and embrace them for the lessons they represent and the Tank could lose the need to always see through every potential pitfall. It is inevitable that the Tank will miss something sometime, and if the Tank does not let go of always needing to be infallible, he or she may miss the joy in discovering new vistas because of the attempt at covering all bets.

# CHAPTER VIII

## HARMONY AT LAST

The biggest challenge of human development will be learning to love and respect our differences. To get beyond the Whirligig and the Tank issue means to make a Giant step toward exercising our potential to the fullest. It is like a huge joke of the Gods to give us this perfect blend of complementary skills, thoughts and talents, and then to make our existence a major struggle of fighting against the very thing that was meant to be a gift.

To gain the gift we must let go. To let go we must give up our ego and become humble with our talents. To give up our ego is the greatest challenge imaginable. To do so means to conquer our deepest and most hidden fears.

The Tank must let go and take imponderable chances with failure. Why does the Tank fear failure so much and what is he or she really giving up in order to trust the Whirligig's magic? Is failure the fear or is the fear a fear of the possibility of being great?

To gain the gift of the Tank, the Whirligig must let go of an insatiable need for freedom and the need to be in control. What is the fear behind this fear? Why is the Whirligig so afraid to trust that his or her destiny could be entwined with another's? Is the Gig afraid he or she will no longer be recognizable by the Gods? Is it perhaps their identity they fear they will lose? Or are the Gigs afraid they won't get the credit for the ideas if they must count on the Tanks to implement them? Do the Tanks believe that because they implemented the idea, they should get the credit?

Each is a soul issue and each is resolvable only at the highest level of introspection. It is the work of a lifetime or even of several lifetimes. For that reason, nothing will change overnight. Perhaps, however, with some discipline and understanding of the differences, we will all bring ourselves, in spite of ourselves, a little closer to perfection.